..

Banjo

SAMANTHA WYNNE-RHYDDERCH has published
two collections, *Rockclimbing in Silk* (Seren, 2001),
and *Not in These Shoes* (Picador, 2008), which was
shortlisted for Wales Book of the Year 2009.

D0756005

Also by Samantha Wynne-Rhydderch

Rockclimbing in Silk

Not in These Shoes

Banjo

Samantha Wynne-Rhydderch

PICADOR

First published 2012 by Picador
an imprint of Pan Macmillan, a division of Macmillan Publishers Limited
Pan Macmillan, 20 New Wharf Road, London N1 9RR
Basingstoke and Oxford
Associated companies throughout the world
www.panmacmillan.com

ISBN 978-0-330-54466-5

Visit **www.picador.com** to read more about all our books
and to buy them. You will also find features, author interviews and
news of any author events, and you can sign up for e-newsletters
so that you're always first to hear about our new releases.

For Geraint

Looking back I realised . . . that those Hut Point days would prove some of the happiest in my life. Just enough to keep us warm, no more – no frills nor trimmings; there is many a worse and more elaborate life. The necessaries of civilisation were as luxuries to us and . . . satisfy only those wants which they themselves create.

Apsley Cherry-Garrard, *The Worst Journey in the World* (Penguin, 1922, p. 206)

It may have been due to the genius of Scott in exercising just the right amount of discipline with a minimum of formality, and even more to the character of Dr. Wilson, the Chief of Scientific Staff. Whatever the reason, this was a happy expedition in spite of the grave disaster that overwhelmed us halfway through. It was significant that in the second winter, when we were reduced to thirteen, life in the hut followed the same pattern as before as far as possible.

Frank Debenham, "An Expedition in Harmony" (*Geographical Magazine*, 1962, 35.1:1–7)

Contents

Banjo

Sewer

White seems an unwise shade for hip waders
but slip into them. Descend the drains,

shafts, intestines of Paris to map
each tunnel onto a boulevard

six storeys up where waiters brush crumbs,
scrawl on chalkboards. Bricks, crypts,

ticks, cracks. Cataphilia is catching
under this city on stilts. Inside

its arteries you're on the run
from a rogue gene, the shake of its tail

at each corner. Catacombs, sewers, cables,
pipes. The rules of the surface world

do not apply. You could hide in galleries,
along corridors of trains, watermains, seams

of bones, but best follow your guide through
cool vaults, flirt under palettes of sediment.

Again. Did you hear it? That's your heart
in plastercast in quarries of gypsum,

wine cellars, reservoirs, canals. Be glad
of ladders, that you're not in splints,

that arms will lift you through the layers
of lumps to scans, ultrasound, blood counts.

Gypo

The turquoise eyes of peacocks' tails
at Powis Castle persuaded me
that pattern matters. So did the geometry
of pink brick twisted chimneys

at Compton Wynyates in whose
knot gardens I found myself
lost and intricate at eight.
I'd memorise visors, Gothic screens,

gables and displays of tapestries.
I could tell a Pembroke
from a Pier table, played
Greensleeves on the recorder

in places where I did not live
but visited in the pages
of *Treasures of Britain*
on a fold-out table in the caravan

where I grew up on the outskirts
of Burnley. In love with the symmetric
pleading of sleeping knights,
brass-necked down to their

pointy toes, I'd cup the faces
of misericords like much-loved dolls,
design chevrons for my family shield,
draw the Queen's buckskin boots

and virginals, squeeze myself into
the chicken run to check I'd still
fit, dreamed one day I'd own a
Ha-ha. Ha ha ha ha ha ha.

Vive la Résistance!

It was on such a night as this that I floated
like a débutante into the arms of a cornfield
outside Rouen, my parachute silks streaming
into a bridal train adorning the corn,

and for the first time felt the full weight
of what it must be to be a woman always
dragging a dress through obtuse fields. So I
unharnessed myself from the lot, rolled up

my folds and ran off to the lych gate
of Sainte Marie du Chêne where I awaited
an assignation with a Monsieur Lefas
who passed me a map in a cigarette packet

which I followed to a farm to be met by
a frowning chap in breeches who unhooked
the door of a barn where his daughter was
hitching up a bed for me in linsey-woolsey.

At the altar, I hovered between doubt
and belief until she glided down the aisle
stitched into my parachute, and for a second
we soared above the priest, the spire,

the higgledy fields, the two of us threaded
together in the silks that had saved me, which I later
unbuttoned and she has since trapped in the attic
in case one day they take off without us.

Dodge

To start off there was winter to consider:
that was no time to rebuild a truck. Match two dots,
button up the rest of the engine and fifty-fifty
you'd be wrong, yes, mama, no matter what
the cookbook says. Then there was the barn: you need

a woodburner at twenty below. The tamarack
is your basic tree in New Hampshire. Up in Maine
they call them hackmatacks. A 1948 Chevy
or a Ford with half a fender found on any
New England farm would do, but in snow country

salt corrosion makes noodle soup out of wiring.
Hell, there's a dozen things you can move
with a blue Dodge 1950 short wheelbase pickup.
Two hundred dollars. I jacked her up, stripped
the chassis till there were no distractions left

but springs and bolts. Black dreck of dog hair,
turnpike receipts, oil molasses-thick beneath
the engine – only part of an automobile
most shade-tree mechanics get. Twenty nuts
torqued down. Hours staring at valves,

reverse thread lug bolts, drive shaft
parking brakes. How is it all the tappets
come off but don't fit back? The manual neglects
to tell me which way the crankshaft rotates
when the engine's running. Pistons pencilled

on the barn wall. A bourbon by the fire
or in the bath. May and my first shake-down cruise
around the block: gear locked, flaps down,
magneto on. After a winter pinned under a truck
I'm heading south, sweetheart. Hop in.

Hong Kong Mah Jong

i.m. Elizabeth Menna Owen Wilders 1915–1996

Twice more the coral trout flicks his tail
on the stone floor of the wet market
in Sheung Wan. Three slits. His heart
squeaks out. Glass cases bubble
with sea bream and painted sweetlip.
Ten pairs of dried squids' eyes crinkle
in baskets on Chung Hom Kok Road.
Red lanterns tease sweat from lychees,

dragonfruit and the jasmine tea
that wreathes our game of Mah Jong.

In his teapot shop one metre deep,
Ken is the protagonist whose show
shivers each time the vans shamble by.
The allure of porcelain whose
brushstroked birds and splash of lotus
I know from home: those twenty-four cups
my great-grandfather stowed

on the *Romanby* – not one cracked –
and a set of Mah Jong lozenges, doll-sized

unopenable books from Mong Kok,
each Chinese letter a forest.
In the Bird Garden scarlet minivets vie
with tiger shrikes to sweeten the air.
Beneath orchids goldfish kiss:
marble lyretail molly, bloodfin terra.
When we unwrapped the box
after six weeks at sea, Dad's
tortoise shuffled towards the light

and died. Seven characters,
four circles, one bamboo.

Alec leaves the olive in his Cosmopolitan
as he slithers in the red and dark
of the bar on the twenty-ninth floor
at La Plaza where I am electrified to see
the Star Ferry creak and wink in a crease
of the South China Sea whose junks
are the size of those Dad folded

into his clothes to fit windowsills at home.
Keep your wind tiles close: West, South, North,

East. The path around the racecourse
is blistered with the roots of candlenut trees,
the grass loved up by English mowers
and hoses. A tram shakes its old bones.
In the souvenir shops on the Peak
the bells on gold pagodas dote
on white jade and lacquer trays
like those New Quay's seafarers

bequeathed to me. Check your flower cards:
plum, camellia or chrysanthemum?

The day the Japanese turned the handle
of the front door of *Fragrant Lagoon*
Aunt Min was re-arranging poinsettias
on the verandah, fixing a gin for Lionel
with lime. Never lemon. In the panels
of their Qing dynasty armoire, the beaks
of the songbirds had been carved

open. Take your pick: Spring, Summer, Autumn
or Winter. Four years inside Stanley Camp.

All that remains are a pair of gloves
whose fingers she'd knitted
from worn-out sweaters, a cream cracker
glazed red, white and blue, still delicious
in her handbag when she died and a menu
for Cinio Cymdeithas Dewi Sant,
St David's Day Dinner 1943: rice,

seeds, roots, rice. Red Dragon, Green
Dragon, White Dragon. Your turn.

Delft

I promise when I pack up the clogs,
raise them to chime with one chipped toe
your passing; when I glue back a pleat
in the skirt of the lady with pale blue hair
whose apron said *B ugge* after she fell
down the stairwell revealing a bell
beneath her dress on which a windmill
was waving goodbye to four birds
reflected in the inky water; when I wrap
the cold tile where your butter flattened
the sheaves of hay combed to a tuft
in the still wind in which etched-in cows
stared out under low clouds looming over
a walled garden whose gate I longed to
walk through always – I promise the glaze
will be wet on all your Delft, on both my hands.

Sharing Your Bed

All night the morning was coming
like the clock said it would.
To make the darkness last
I held your right hand tight.
You won't remember the weight
of my fingers warming yours.
As the tocks ticked by
you were losing your grip,
criss-crossing in your dream
the String Road to Lochranza,
blonde as your hair
rivering down the pillow.
Above your bed the red boat rocked
back and fore, back and fore
beside the bridge in the painting
you'd loosened with water
and brushes years ago. And I knew
because the clock told me so
that morning was coming
and that you would have to go.
I thought of macramé as you twisted
your hands in mine, of the twine
and hemp you'd pull
into reverse half-hitches. All night
I plaited my fingers into yours
like a Pagoda Knot to pull you through
the morphine sleep, to keep you

under this roof. You breathed
and breathed until by dawn you had
no more breaths to weave
no more cords to tauten
and I, your child, woke beside you
holding a lattice of stiff fingers.

No Good at Fruit

And worse, she has forgotten how to dig,
widowed at the brink of this window
of land, twelve foot square allotted

by the council, one for each of their quota
of years. If she stares long enough, courgettes
will grow, yes, the small heat of a cloche

console her, that transparent hat on a pout of chard.
At least, that's all she can make out from here
with only a quarter of her vision left.

She can't see his strawberries rotting, the nets
pinning them down, down, staking a claim
for him. Outside his shed, the plums sit

like unripe tears in her hand. The sun strikes
six lilies, her blaze of white. She has a plot:
she'll turn it all over to dahlias – yes, a bedspread

of *Lauren Michelles* and *Castle Drives*
that she will see from upstairs on summer nights
while the horseshoe still smiles above the door.

Table Manners

Let's have you sitting straight. Your relationship with
furniture comes first. Don't be marooned
at the linen's edge: etiquette's a dialect
to help. Hold your napkin like an injured bird

then unfurl its water lily to quilt your lap.
Keep a candle to the centre of the map,
gerbera to your right, unless, that is, you've
anything to hide, in which case,

make it two. Do not remove your shoes or
show any flesh. Tilt your soup's light towards
her, like an invitation to swim. Sip
as though you're working on it. Elbows off!

If she asks for salt, remember pepper's
meant. Don't stare. Set your smile to
simmer. Stand when a lady leaves. If you catch
yourself distorted in a fork, do not fret

with the cruet or a match; we don't leave marks
except on glass. Cutlery is a code. If your
implements kiss on the plate this indicates
you're after more. Ten to five means it's over.

Stuffed

This glass case is typical Hutchings:
bun feet, gilded strips, classic snarl,
blood on the teeth. The recipe of choice
in nineteenth century preservation
was white arsenic, chalk and soap
in equal parts; seabirds best skinned
through an incision under the wing
to hide seepage. Polecats, stoats
or otters – they'd all be wired
to pounce, pins holding their coats
in place. Mine's an ambush case:
a fox peering over a ledge

at the throat of a rabbit. It was fur
I thought of at four in the morning
one night last March when a key
turned in the glass-fronted cabin
I'd rented for peace for a week
in a forest (no curtains, better view)
and as I hid behind the claw foot bath
I heard beating in my blood a line
from Conan Doyle, *from the find
to the kill*, that I'd learnt as a child
under the monkey puzzle tree,
and the two men pawing at my door.

Ladies with Hammers

i.m. Mary Anning 1799–1847

The trick is not to lift your gaze
above the waist in case you miss

a pattern in the quilted cliffs in which
the cup and saucer of a croc's eye

might catch your own. Nor be distracted by
a colonel buttoned up by his desire

to collect and classify, consign to
cabinets his bezoars and ammonites

all the while scanning your chest to check
your curiosities or your scruffy gloves

to see if shells are all you're selling.
Social strata collapse when you're

scrabbling on the seashore. Went out
fossilising yesterday with Lucy Oates.

Although we spoke only of pentacrinites
and grypheas I'm sure she has been

crossed in love. Fossils are bodies
that have turned to stone. You must take care

when chipping away at clay not to
precipitate a landslip. I have tripped up

more than once and as a consequence
live on display among these shelves of brittle stars.

For the Love of Rust

It begins with a blush
across the tin roof
of a lean-to, crimped auburn
by the affection of autumn.
A shingle shangle
of dripping rust
disturbs
this September afternoon,
turning crimson
in its desire
to disintegrate,
a trace
of bitten lace.
Let corrosion corrugate us
as we conjugate *conrodere:*
to go red together
until an endless letter S
ripples ochre
through the spectrum of vermilion
all along the edge
of the barn's upturned curve
under which I shimmer
in the rope of your arms.
Here's how.

Harbour Dues

I'm falling in love with the pier,
the curve of its spine and its uneven teeth,

with its litany printed on clapboard, a speech
in rhyme, a guide to the obsessions

of nineteenth century clerks,
a memorial whose edicts I recite in my sleep:

the shillings owed for unloading
every hundredweight of feathers,

of hemp and flax, saltpetre, gunpowder,
for cigars (per box), for ivory and horn,

every crate of figs and French prunes,
every calf, pig or fox, every bundle

of laths except rosewood and ebony,
for every butt of ale, cider and perry,

every ton of culm, coal, limestone and zinc,
every bushel of onions, every chest of tea,

cocoa, treacle, molasses and cheese,
every quarter of wheat, malt, pease

and tares, every barrel of pitch, tar or tallow,
every cask of butter, for candles

and soap, every plough or harrow,
for every wardrobe, card table, pianoforte,

barrel organ, bath chair and sofa,
which reminds me – you still owe me

for that three-piece suite I shipped out
to New Jersey in time for last Christmas.

The Language of Doors

If you have leaned back full tilt
in a rocking chair on a verandah
by moonlight, pulled your coat closer
beneath the balustrade's ramblings
as the wind lays itself at your feet
like a performance about to begin –

then you'll have given in to splayed shingles,
confessed to raking cornices that you are
in fact a clapboard-and-quoins kind of girl
who goes for low-pitched hip roofs,
lunettes, fretwork, reglets on Cape Cods,
that rafter tails are not for you,

nor self-effacing façades nor numbered kits
of Foursquares shipped by Sears Roebuck,
nor the syllables fluent in glass over the porch:
Araminta, Zenobia, Bamenda, Claremont,
that Stick Style's your thing, sawtooth trims
and beaded-board soffits, that you adore a house
for its lintels and plinths, its chevrons and shells.

40 Hampton Road

The hedge fought back
as we'd force our way through
to the stream that whispered to
my red boat on the jaunty rocks.

Under the clock's frown we'd sprinkle
hundreds of thousands of hundreds
and thousands. The twins pointed their
pas de deux at the piano we banged

after tea. *Dave*, said the pebbledash
under the windowsill when I'd watch
my sister squeal water all over
the raspberries. *Anna Loves Dave*

glinted the veiny stones. I'd try the handle
to the balcony. Locked again. It was
unsafe, you see. When I first heard
the news I thought that was the door

the murderer had picked. But he was
already in the house. She died
in my bed twenty years after I left.
With her mother. Here we all are,

lined up. In front of the raspberry bushes.
Her father. Point blank. In the head.
I'm the little one at the end, yes.
Look: sticky hands.

Tomahawk

i.m. Sarah Margaret Rhydderch Davies 1905–1989

Feel the blade just here
at the tip. See the nicks in the flint?
If you squint at its shaft sheathed in red felt

and eagle feathers a squiggled inscription
tells the story of sky-tinted water,
a deep creek called Shenandoah

my great-grandpa refused to leave
so his daughter fled with her beads
to a white man. Name of Davies,

trading firearms out of the Plains.
If you keep the Cree Ghost Dance
she's written on the back

of the only photograph we have,
the earth will return to the Indians.
By the time my father lifted

the tomahawk, it had been handed down
three generations of the tribe.
As a child in their little reservation

in Aberarth, he waltzed its blade into
a leg of their shed on stilts,
his sister jiving inside.

Emigré

Let me cradle this stiff body
one more time before I lay it
in a velvet bed. I've no mind to pin

its strings to the fingerboard
or coax the blond hair of a bow
over its bony shoulders, this, the only
companion of your narrow bunk

in steerage on the voyage out,
and on the barstool down the cobbled lane
where you sank your last glass

of porter the hour you boarded,
at one with the swing of the ship,
tapping out a jig in three-four time
as the engine crooned ahead.

When you were startled by a sea-flute
swooning through the camisoles
she'd strung between bunks

you made music all the way
to Ellis Island. I am custodian
all the way back of your silent violin
and this, a doll-sized coffin.

ERRATICS

Doorly

Gerald Doorly: Third Officer, SY *Morning*, supply ship to
Captain Scott's *Discovery* expedition (1901–1904)

THE PIANO

for Louise & Joe

In a jangle of harnesses she arrived late
at the quayside, so we left her out on deck
for a week with the ice picks and coal sacks

until the Sunday we steamed into Biscay.
Neither door to the wardroom would admit
her maple ribs so the Chief Engineer cut her

in half with the Cook's meat saw. Grease helped.
Each string quivered as we unshipped
the keyboard. She braced herself

beneath the rigging, her hitch pins visible,
her struts jumpy. I passed the afternoon with Evans
handing her parts down, glueing her back,

inserting dowels. My tuning lever twisted easily
inside her. Later we were all over her
for a minstrelsy, blacked up in burnt cork

until a squall rolled the vessel thirty degrees.
We trampled the camp stools of our mock stalls
in red cummerbunds and oakum wigs

in the rush to take in the top-gallants. She
screeched across the wardroom floor,
her back tense against my cabin door.

SWIVEL

The seats in the wardroom are revolving
mahogany, speaking in creaks wherever we go,
basket weave for the tropics,
leather for the cold. We cross decks

in mess dress without spilling a drink
from England to Africa, New Zealand
and back, waltzing through the Forties
as low as we dare to the swish of pack ice,

the intimacy of days full of night.
We can't permit our chairs to strut
south through the swell. We nail
their feet to the floor. They arch

their backs to protest, all bone on show,
flaunt wicker and brass. At dinner
we keep them well under control.
Ignore their cries – all they need's

a good oiling. Spin to the officer on your left
at hors d'oeuvres, right for the mains,
dead ahead at dessert – but first
twist again on your reversible chairs.

CABLE-KNIT

Landed the tender amid a bedlam of penguins
at Cape Adare where Captain Colbeck

clasped the records of *Discovery*'s route
at Christmas last. He was stitched up to the neck

in the intricacies of his sweetheart's cable-knit
by which she'd moored herself to him

the day the *Morning* cast off. I'd sewed my own.
Bespoke. To re-stock a ship you must first

locate her: notes of her proposed
course were to be roped to red posts

so they'd show against snow. A needle
in the proverbial, as the land's either uncharted

or inaccessible. Meta-cabling comprises
three-cable plaits containing two-cable strands.

In such cases the inner cables sometimes
go their separate ways. Like Lucy and I.

I am still shocked by the electricity
of her hair through my hands. Two cables

should cross each other in a single row.
A spacer row helps the fabric to relax.

The penguins, late for dinner at Cape Crozier,
got into a flap over our winter livery

of turtlenecks as they interrogated
a crimson cylinder inside which curled

an account of the ship's whereabouts
three months ago. Semaphored back

we'd tracked her down to McMurdo Sound.
At midnight's daylight, her masts stark

across ten miles of ice, we sledged over
a ton of apples sweetening slowly

in the hold, passed round port and yarns.
Cable braids are when you tailor

the centre lines on sweaters to alter the course
of the crests and troughs of each cable's wave.

A one-cable serpentine snakes, whereas a two-cable
undulates. A five-cable braid, I elaborated

over brandy, is called a *Celtic Princess*,
interwoven like Mary Lou's locks when I unravel

the weight of their ladder to climb all the way
up her back to the mouth of her yes.

PRINTING PRESS

Each letter is curled in a separate bed
in the type case like a cutaway of the ship's cabins
in miniature, every swirl of the alphabet
carved for its own role. We all hold

two jobs: Wilson is doctor and taxidermist
who's obsessed his sketches won't reflect
the true hues of Antarctica after a winter
in artificial light. With Shackleton, sub-lieutenant

and editor of *The South Polar Times*, he turns out
the playbills and results of football matches
on the floe in letterpress, binds the paper
in Venesta plywood from packing cases.

Reverse relief: as they can't obliterate
the stencilled titles of the original contents
each volume is by default called *The Julienne Soup*,
The Bottled Fruit and *The Irish Stew*.

Clissold

Thomas Clissold: Cook, SY *Terra Nova* RYS,
Captain Scott's last expedition (1910–1913)

CROSSING THE LINE

I'd started to sweat inside the bearsuit
the day we kissed the Equator goodbye,
felt the fur I'd been issued with fit
as if there were no getting out now.
We were halfway there, the itch to reach
the Pole postponed by a day's jolly japes.

Permission to board, sir! At 1.15
Neptune in the person of Evans dripped
onto the foredeck and I shimmied aft
behind the barber, the barrister and his wife
to the break of the poop where Levick
was lathered in soot, shaved and tipped

backwards into the slap of the bath –
a sail full of water slung to starboard –
where we bears were waiting to finish
them off with tickles. No escape.
Underway again by the time we toasted
the sung mauve of southern skies.

The Minstrels at Minus Sixty

A butler is a must. As is a vicar,
a maid, two policemen and a decanter

on a silver tray. The suspect's wife
will be on the buxom side with ruffles

at the neck and cuff, even if
you're so far south of the equator

in a field of ice your only audience
can be the ship's complement

and silence for miles towards the Pole.
We've all had our faces blacked

for the stage at least once: Lashley's
your man there. You need to stay

on good terms with a stoker at sixty
below. Three sweaters beneath petticoats

and tails, we grow into roles larger
than the life we left by the clematis

over the porch at dusk. I keep going back
to that night in The Hut: the Captain

laughed so much his tears froze
to jewels as we flounced back

to the ship, all rouged up and powdered
with flour. Oh you've no need to worry

about me, love, I've no taste
for disguise except in finnesko

and senegraes for sledging: suits me.
You could bury me in that get-up.

BLACKOUT

In all the world there is no desolation more complete
than the Polar night.
Alfred Lansing, *Endurance*

A red bulb. Ma belle tinkling. I whip
the drape from the Bordel to smell
bread rising in the galley. Outside
it's been the wrong side of minus forty-five

for four months. I coax the dough
slow and alive in its chilly tin, skulk
in my bunk until above my head
the bread's Morse says it's ready

for the stove. Dough grows; tilts disc;
lead ball tells bell to blitz pulley and wire
to flash its amber at me. Did this
baking lark begin with knots and threads?

It brings out the Heath Robinson
in me. That's what Simpson whispers,
his anemometer moaning at each gust
all the wordless darkness long.

Birdie

Henry 'Birdie' Bowers: Third Officer,
SY *Terra Nova* RYS (1910–1913)

PONTING

In the end we turned him into a verb:
to pont meaning *to pose in ice and snow*

until frozen. On the voyage south he'd be
tilting plates in the darkroom, in one hand

the developing dish, in the other a basin
of vomit. One minute he'd arrange us

in groups for the cinematograph, then rush
to the ship's side. Once Ponco roped up

his JA Prestwich over *Terra Nova*'s bow,
balanced on three planks. He lost the tip

of his tongue when it stuck to the camera
at thirty below. Corneas can freeze

to peep-sight. At one hundred degrees
of frost the film's ribbon will split.

To pont would also mean *pontificate*. He'd insist
on reeling the film slowly to prevent

sparks. We'd rehearse the Pole Picture:
mount the camera on the theodolite tripod,

wind twine over the trigger and guide it
round a ski stick to get the direction right.

He'd instruct us on setting the shutter, how to
use a flash in the tent with quarter of an inch of powder

and f11. En route to the Pole I sent back
negatives with the support teams, a sheet

torn from my sledging log detailing exposure
data; how composed we were, how cold.

MIND HOW YOU GO

A word from 81¼° south
to tell you how the snow
is sculpted into doves,
in love with the wind;
how there is only enough hay
to take eight of the ponies
up to the foot of the Glacier
where they'll be shot
for dog food; how I'm enclosing
a letter for mother begging her
again to forget that when she
waved me off at Waterloo
a truckload of coffins lay waiting
on the platform; how the wire
we stretched to telephone
from Hut Point to Cape Evans
with time-sights taken by the stars
stopped Scott's vowels
when he rang for Tryggve
to ski over with the Union Jack
we'd left on a desk; how I read
a novel discarded there
in 1909 whose last five pages
were missing and we all tried
to guess the ending.

CURTAIN CALL

We've been taking it in turns
to undo our shirts

in minus seventy to nurse
Oates's frostbitten foot

on our breasts. Jokes in the tent
are discouraged since even laughing

hurts. Yesterday I threw a cup
of boiling tea into the air

to see it freeze before it hit
the ice. If I breathe near a sheet

of my diary the pencil slips
across its polished page as if

I'm writing in a book of glass.
Our clothes crackle

like suits of armour.
We have to play the game

of statues to hear each other
speak. The hardest part

so far was ruffling
the mane of each pony

before we shot them
on the Barrier. Every night

our sleeping bags solidify
to slabs of granite.

Cherry

Apsley Cherry-Garrard: Assistant Zoologist,
SY *Terra Nova* RYS (1910–1913)

MY YEAR OUT

More than the company of girls
I missed colour until my hyacinth bulbs

bloomed blue in a basin of sawdust.
I discovered I could skin a petrel,

loved a lantern chat, but never
got used to sleeping alongside

five empty bunks for a year or guessed
I'd be nailing shut a small box

of each missing man's possessions
or forgot the day we heard a crack

like a shot: Scott's arm breaking
as Atch freed his diary. It was only back

in the developing tank in the darkroom
that we saw our companions

swim towards us from the Pole, blink
in its milky light, walk from the stiff

chrysalis of film that had lain
eight months beside their indigo skin.

BOOTLACES

When we soothed out the bamboo poles
to blanket their bodies with the tent,
next to Scott's face lay traces
of a lashing made out of lamp wick
from his reindeer skin boots, singed
at one end where he'd burned
the remaining spirit from the primus
as light by which to write his final lines.

GEOLOGY

I wish I could say I'd been the kind of child
who collected fossils, who'd turn a stone over
to wonder how those wavy layers had crystallised

into such designs I'd want to sketch
their quiet lines. But I'd pass them all by,
the shales and porphyries, my feet

barely touching the lawn, reaching
for the shuttlecock, the Earl Grey. We dug out
the quartz that had been Scott, Wilson

and Bowers, their lithologies in rock sequence
and the sledge weighed down by thirty-five pounds
of granite they'd stopped to collect from a moraine

on the way back. Erratics: rocks that differ
from those native to where they're found.

LAST MARCH

Dear Daddy
I want
to be a
drummer
when I
grow up
love Peter.

IN SILVER BROMIDE

The string is invisible which Bowers tugged
to include himself in the final photograph
of the five in furs beside a Union Jack's
slap in the face. For months the ink stilled
in the frozen pages, the silk flag stiffened
to a handkerchief in Scott's breast pocket
until their bodies were sifted from the drifts
that held the tin cylinder of negatives –
a small black wound in all that white.

Marston

George Marston: Artist, SY *Endurance*, which sank in
the Weddell Sea ice in Antarctica in November 1915
during Shackleton's Imperial Trans-Antarctic Expedition
(1914–1916)

ARTIST IN RESIDENCE

The bouquet of hair I'm holding in my lap
is my own. That's Wild with the razor. To his right
Crean bites a pipe in black and white. Too dark out
for the dogs that day so we had our hair cut
in the Ritz. Don't we look a bunch of convicts?
As the locks fell I'd soothe each tuft
as if about to dip a horsehair tongue
into magenta or forest green, smell the pine
shedding its fringe at my feet, decode the script
of its bark, still sharp in Hampshire.
The whole of my work went down with that ship
except eight drawings. It was then
my tubes of oils were commandeered
to seal the seams of the three rowing boats
by which we made our escape. Saved by paint.

SAVING THE PLATES

Into which ripped window of the sinking deckhouse,
under whose cabin, beside what half-jammed door,
through whose quarters in the forecastle,
crouching along which handrail to escape

the sub-zero black water, in which passageway
of that jilted ship did Hurley inch towards
the cupboard where his glass plates lay encased,
all six hundred of them about to skate

down the layers to a sub-glacial lake before
he was forced to stop some twelve feet short
of the darkroom door, give himself up to an icy slush

waist-deep in salt-cellars, cups and split timbers
to salvage seventy negatives and stow those icons
black on white, white on black, into an open boat and row?

Taking Occultations on Elephant Island

The best part of my war so far
has been the nights with Worsley

observing the local time at which
the moon obscures the Southern Cross.

But he's left me for an 850-mile journey
on the *Caird* to South Georgia

to get help. And he's taken the sextant.
If you trace a line from Alpha and Gamma,

and extend it 4.5 times the distance
between the two stars you'll be close

to the Southern Celestial Pole.
He's navigating by the stars we know

and love while I am joining the dots
of their bright writing, the constellation's

inclination from the perpendicular
to calculate the present time which

indicates any day now I will decry
his ship and say goodbye to all this.

Hussey

Leonard Hussey: Meteorologist,
SY *Endurance* (1914–1916)

BUNTING

Our knitwear glitters on ropes
between tents. Sledge pennants
spell their reds and greens

across Antarctica's inscrutable white,
clap as we scalp a seal. In the light
of a blubber lamp we juggle

rations of tinned spinach and suet
from floe to floe as cracks in the ice
track us down. Weeping this evening

in no. 5 tent at the loss
of their dearly-beloved Colonel
who feels the need to sleep

in the galley tent until the caravan
rolls on (he doubles up
as culinary consultant) but he'll

join us for charades at half-past.
I shall think of 1915
as my year in the circus,

our very own carnival on ice.
Last time I followed a float
I was *A Little Nut Tree* holding hands

with *Twinkle Twinkle Little Star*,
my brother who's most likely
joined up. All we can see

of the ship that was our home
is the top of her funnel
sinking through floes, struggling

to give the performance of her life,
her wire rigging writing
goodbye in the ice.

In My Arms

You must hold her for ten minutes
every night for a week, embrace
the weight of her head, slide your hand
the length of her neck, let her rest
between your legs, counting

each fret down to the flick
of her tailpiece before you even
pluck a note so you and your banjo
become one, in tune for life.
Hey, don't strum. Only a year before

the Antarctic trip I'd been serenading
cannibals in the Sudan. That's where I learnt
three-finger picking and Minstrel Hits:
Swannee River, Massa's in De Cold
Cold Ground. After six months'

floating on ice floes we upturned
two rowing boats to pitch our home
on Elephant Island. A chronometer case
doubled as window. Evenings round the stove
with Mick faking the trombone:

Old Dan Tucker, the Rannee Hooley Blues.
The photograph shows
the most motley crew of troubadours
that ever was projected on a plate.
A two-gallon petrol can played urinal.

For many a mile it's the most
palatial dwelling place you'll find
on Hell-of-an-Isle. Toasts with meths
most nights in July till that supply
dwindled too. All the boys inscribed

their names on my banjo's skin.
Back in London I hung her above the desk
in my practice so I could treasure
her stretch marks for ever, cherish
those five strings that made me sing.

GREENHEART

Sipiroe and *bibiru* are the names my father used for
    Demerara Greenheart
in Guyana, its timber too tough to cut with an adze.
    Twenty-six inches of it
parted my cabin bed from the frozen seas which
    squeezed the ship in their grip
like a nut. At the first bite of the ice every man
    on *Endurance* felt as though

he himself had been touched. You'd hear it crack
    like distant artillery
as the floes fought out a border, tenting up into
    starched hedgerows
until 18th October 1915 when they wedged into her
    port beam. She heeled
thirty degrees. Below deck every ladle, picture and
    curtain hung

as if caught in a high wind all along the starboard
    bulkhead. She sighed
from midships forwards in a brash tangle of masts
    and ropes until
the ice swallowed her whole: her English Elm, her
    Pitch Pine, her Riga Fir
her Indian Teak, her Honduras Mahogany, her
    Dantzic Oak, her Greenheart.

ACKNOWLEDGEMENTS

I am grateful to Naomi Boneham, archivist at the Scott Polar Research Institute (SPRI) in Cambridge, and Shirley Sawtell, librarian at SPRI, the Scott family for giving me permission to view Scott's correspondence with his wife, Kathleen, Discovery Point Museum in Dundee, Stephen Scott-Fawcett for kindly giving me a compact disc of the *Songs of the Morning*, Louise and Joe Bugeja for dissecting their piano, Margaret Atkins and the community and staff at Boarbank Hall for a room with a view, Lilwen Lewis, Sara Lewis and Richard Steenberg for reading the earliest versions of the Antarctic poems, Liz Kristiansen for showing me her uncle Jack Ashton's Antarctic photographs, Matthew Francis and the Aberystwyth Poetry Group for commenting on some of these poems, Polly Clark for mentoring on the Fielding Programme, my cousin, Guy Passmore, for showing me footage of an auction of Scott memorabilia, my sister, Melody Emmerson, for lending me her copy of *The Worst Journey in the World* by Apsley Cherry-Garrard, my sister, Francesca Rhydderch, for her unstinting encouragement, Kate Clanchy for her boundless generosity and patience in reading versions of these poems, my editor, Don Paterson, for his thoughtful comments, Literature Wales for awarding me a bursary to enable me to write the first part of this collection and to the editors of the following publications where some of these poems first appeared: *Agenda*, *Magma*, the *Edinburgh Review*, *New Welsh Review*, *Planet*, *Poetry London*, *Poetry Wales* and *Best British Poetry 2011* ed. Roddy Lumsden (Salt, 2011).